How to Text Your Ex Boyfriend Back

Get Your Ex Back in 6 Simple Steps

~ James J. Ryan

Disclaimer

Table of Contents

Yes You Can Get Your Ex Back

Hi, my name is J. J. Ryan (just J.J. to my friends),

I wanted to say thanks for grabbing a copy of my book, *"How to Text Your Ex Boyfriend Back: Get Your Ex Back in 6 Simple Steps"*

This book contains proven steps and strategies on how to use simple text messages to lure your man back to you and have him begging to be yours again.

These are simple powerful techniques to cut past the facade he's thrown up to avoid you. You'll be able to insert ideas into his mind that he won't be able to let go of and he'll think of over and over again. By using your ex's existing emotions "against them" you'll be able to get the positive result you want. Move past your old relationship and into a new one with this amazing process for texting your ex back.

Let's get started!

The Rainbow after the Rain

Regardless of age, getting your heart broken is one of the most difficult things that you have to deal with. Having someone walk out of your life after years of happy moments together, is never an easy thing to go through. Crying at night and dreading to wake up in the morning are just among the normal consequences of having your heart broken. You might even feel hopeless at times. There will be days when you will feel desperate and you would want to go marching to your ex-boyfriend's house to get back together. And, there will be days when all you want to do is crawl back into your bed and mope. Your friends will try their best to cheer you up but sometimes, their encouraging words and company will not suffice. You are going through a breakup – and you feel the worst of the emotions. But don't fret. You are not alone.

All of us have gone through break ups – good ones, bad ones, relieving ones and awful ones. Breaking up with someone is never easy, especially if you are the one who was left behind. Aside from your self-esteem going down on an all-time low, you also tend to feel guilty. You think that you caused the break up. After countless bottles of beer and ice cream tubs, you will end up thinking that everything was your fault. You will hate yourself. And for the nth time, you will break down.

The cycle is normal. But before you totally bury yourself in despair, consider this one fact: we all have lost someone we love before but the good thing is that we can always fight to have them back.

Just because the story ended does not mean you can just leave it as is. You may have caused the break up or you might be the one left behind, but if you feel that your love story deserves another shot, you can try again – you can always get back together with your ex-boyfriend. But to succeed, there are things you have to do before you can have him back into your arms.

Making sure that you get another shot into working out your relationship is not as easy as it sounds. You have to plan your every move wisely so that you would successfully pull him back into your life and not push him further away. Luckily, today's technology makes it easier and less awkward for a girl to do this. Gone are the days when it would be embarrassing for a girl to beg a boy to return to their relationship. Nowadays, you can mend your relationship through text messages. However, you have to be cautious about what messages to send, when to send them and how exactly you would send them. At this time, it is very important for you to observe relationship politics. And lastly, you have to make sure that you always play your cards right.

Step One: Do Not Text

Yes, you read it right. Most girls commit the worst mistake of texting their ex-boyfriends right after their break up. Avoid this at all cost. No matter how lonely the nights have become or how badly you want to be with your ex-boyfriend, do not send him a message.

When you break up with someone, there is a normal tendency of wanting to fix things right away. It is very common for girls to think that they can mend things after just a few hours. They think that if they act on the situation early, they can lessen the damage and the relationship would not fail. These girls would call back their ex-boyfriends countless of times or drive to their houses so that they would get a chance to talk. They would do everything they can to get a hold of their ex-lovers and despite these grand gestures, this would not work. As a matter of fact, it might even push the guys away.

It is understandable that girls can get depressed when they go through a breakup. They cry buckets of tears, eat lots of ice cream and sometimes refuse to get out of their sweatpants. These are normal things that girls do when they are heartbroken and these are reasonable. If you are heartbroken, you can do these things, too. Do whatever will make you feel better – just do not reach out to your ex-boyfriend. Do not follow him everywhere, do not stalk his Facebook profile and the most important of them all, do not text him.

Ironically, the first rule in texting your way back to your ex-boyfriend's life is by not texting him.

There is no exact time frame as to how long you should be banned from texting. The duration sometimes depends on how grave the break up was, the reasons for it or if there are no other circumstances and people involved. Sometimes, it is best to forego the texting for about two weeks when the break up was only caused by a misunderstanding. Some people go through the no-text period for as long as three months because there was still a need to settle issues first before fixing the relationship. However, most people suggest that a 30-day period of no texting should suffice.

After the break up, you should do everything in your power to avoid texting your ex-boyfriend. A whole month of no text (or any other forms of communication) is strictly advised. And because we all went through break ups before, we know that this is not easy to accomplish. You have been with the guy for months or years, stopping the communication would be a great deviation from your usual routine. But you should.

The 30-day hiatus is a good period for you to think things over. You can cry about the separation, you can listen to sad songs until you get sick and tired of them, you can evaluate what really happened or you can reflect on where things started to go wrong. This time will be a great chance for you to reflect and heal. Some girls who go through break ups and follow the no-text period use this time to mope around and feel sorry for themselves. At this time, it is still understandable so you might want to take advantage of the situation. During the first days, your friends will understand why you would not want to go out or why you pity yourself too much. They will not judge you for crying every night or for starting fights with them every single time that they say you deserve better. Your friends will let this behavior pass for the first weeks but after that, you will have to fix yourself and move on with your life –no matter how you plan to do this.

During this one month ordeal, it is also encouraged that you work on making yourself better. Do the things you were not able to do when you were still in a relationship. Go to the gym, enroll in a class, hang out with your friends or start a new hobby. If you were restricted by your ex-lover to travel because he was the jealous type or because he could not be with you, this will be a great time to go through with your plans. Explore different places, learn new cultures and meet other people. Do everything that will make you happy. This is your chance to work on yourself. Enjoy being single for 30 days before you go back to being in a relationship. It is best to give yourself a breather from all the stress and emotions that your break up has brought you.

If you are still itching to grab that phone and send an emotional text, stop yourself and have a trusty friend to save you instead. We suggest that whenever you feel like texting your ex-boyfriend, you text this friend instead. It is encouraged that you choose your best friend to be this person because she will be the one who will understand you the most. She will not judge you for texting emotional messages or she will not scold you for even trying to reach out to your ex-boyfriend. Also, there are some girls who opt to text the messages to their friends instead. In a way, they have released whatever they wanted to say, even if the person to whom they sent it was not the person they wanted to send it to. Try doing this. Whenever you feel lonely and would want to talk to your ex-boyfriend, whether to question him or to relieve old happy memories, you can create a message and send it to your friend instead. It may not be the same as talking to your ex-boyfriend but it will make you feel a bit better.

But of course, banning you from texting your former lover also means that you should avoid "accidentally" bumping into him. Some girls tend to get a bit desperate that they would go to the usual places they used to go to or the places they know where their ex-boyfriends will be. Do not do this. Do not make the world smaller for you two after the break up. Instead, avoid going to these places. Instead, use the space and time apart to cool your heads.

After the break up, the best thing you could do is to wait. Wait until the 30-day period is over. By then, you would have a clearer mind and stable emotions. Aside from saving yourself from embarrassment or rejection, this 30-day period also helps you become a better version of yourself so it is actually a win-win situation. Furthermore, this period will make your ex-boyfriend wonder why you haven't reached out. This will keep him thinking whether you have found someone else or if you still miss him. This confusion will be particularly helpful to you in the succeeding steps in getting your ex-boyfriend back.

Step Two: Be Casual and Cool

After you survive that 30-day period, it is now time to text your ex-boyfriend. As mentioned, by the end of this period, you should have already worked on your emotions; you have a clearer point of view with what happened to your relationship; and of course, you already know how you want to get your ex-boyfriend back. After that month long hiatus, you can now reach out to your ex-lover. But what exactly should you tell him in your text message? Step Two requires you to be casual and cool in your text messages.

Texting your ex-boyfriend after weeks of no communication at all can be tricky. You may want to beg him to get back together with you or you may want to tell him how much you missed him. This is normal but you have to control yourself. Do not act on these feelings. You should keep your first text simple, short and casual.

Aside from choosing your words wisely, you should also be cautious as to when you will send the message. Never send your message late at night or early in the morning. Texting late at night connotes that you are lonely and he is the person you are thinking of. When you text him early in the morning, he may also get the impression that he was the first thought of your day. Although these may be true, you would not want him to think this. Instead, you may want to send him a casual message in the middle of the day. Texting during your lunch break or during your coffee break is preferable.

At this point, you may want to know what exactly a "casual" text message is. To give you an idea, here are three casual messages that you may want to consider sending:

1. "Hey, I saw your friend Mike today. I heard you guys went to LA over the summer."

The best reason to text your ex-boyfriend is because you bumped into his friend or relative. Your ex-boyfriend will not think of anything else other than you sent a message because someone made you remember him and not because you terribly miss him. The good thing about this kind of text is that you will not come across as desperate to talk to him. You just happened to see his friend and that is it.

But of course, if you send this kind of text, be sure that this really happened. Do not pretend to have seen his sister or his friend somewhere. Chances are he would ask these people if you really did see them. If this did not happen, you will not just become desperate in his eyes but you will also be labelled as a liar. Save yourself from both embarrassment and rejection, do not make up stories.

2. "I just finished reading this book and I thought you may want to read it, too. It's science fiction."

When your ex-boyfriend receives this kind of text, he would wonder why you sent him a message. He would have different interpretations of your message: "Is she texting me because she thought of me while reading the book?" or "Is she texting me because she wants to communicate again?" Your ex-boyfriend will surely be confused and this is a good thing.

When you text your ex-boyfriend, choose a topic that you know he would not ignore. In this second example, the sender and her ex-boyfriend are avid fans of books so she sent him a message about them, particularly about science fiction. You should do the same. If your ex-boyfriend is into other things such as cars or basketball, use this as a subject of your text.

Also, you may observe from the text message above that the sender did not mention the book title. This is a great tactic. The reason why she did not tell the title right away is because there will be a need for the ex-boyfriend to reply to ask the name of the book. By not completing the details of the book, there is a better chance of having the message replied to.

3. "I discovered a good nachos place. Check it out at the 23rd Street."

And of course, a good casual text is short. This third example is very friendly and does not invite any other interpretation other than you sharing your latest discovery. Make your text short so that you would not seem too eager to talk to him. Text him in a way that you would normally text your friends about something you just learned.

Once you have sent in your casual text, you should also be prepared for whatever he may reply. It is normal that he would start a conversation with you. He would ask how you are doing and what you have been up to lately. It is okay to answer these questions but you may want to avoid telling him how miserable you have been in the last few weeks or how much you missed talking to him. Do not give in. Keep your guards up. Answer as casual as possible and end the conversation early. By doing these, you will keep him guessing and wanting more.

Step Three: Walk Down Memory Lane

Now that you guys are communicating once again, it would be advisable that you bring back the good times so that he will be reminded of how great you guys were together. However, you should not just open up the topic whenever you feel like doing so. The success of this third step mainly relies on timing. This may be crucial for some because it can sometimes be difficult to determine if the timing is right or if it is better to keep your mouth shut for a while. Fortunately for you, we will provide you the three easy steps into bringing up the good memories into the conversation:

1. When you casually talk to your ex-boyfriend, try not to start the conversation with any topic or any particular subject relating to your relationship. Instead, try to open up a conversation with something random, such as a common friend or a common hobby. By talking about something else or something informal and casual, you will put your guy at ease and he will feel comfortable talking to you.

2. Now that he is comfortable, you can start with the hints. For instance, if you guys are big baseball fans, you may want to start with something insignificant but related to baseball. Texting things like "I heard your team won the game last Saturday" or "I saw the latest scores, your team is doing good!" are excellent way to provide hints. Once your guy is immersed into the conversation, you can begin the walk down memory lane.

3. A text saying "Remember that time we watched that game and we ended up laughing the whole night?" is a good way to relive the past. When you are trying to reminisce with your guy through text, it is advised that you do not just give all the details away. Just open the conversation and let him follow your lead, that way he will be forced to remember on his own. When he tries to recall those occasions, it is expected that he will feel nostalgic. Through this simple reminiscing, he will definitely remember how good he had it with you.

By following these three easy steps, you are easily on your way to getting back the love of your life!

Step Four: Juggle Emotions with Jealousy

At this point, it can be safely assumed that you have played your cards right because not only have you ignited your ex-boyfriend's interest but you have also maintained your communication through text messages. But do not feel victorious just yet. The fourth step in getting back together with your ex may be the trickiest of them all and will require you to be extra cautious. This fourth step is considered too delicate because you will have to play with your ex-boyfriend's emotions.

Although you may be in constant communication with your guy, there is no guarantee that he will be getting back together with you. There is no concrete way of finding out if he is in for the long run but there are ways to know if there is a chance. Making your ex-boyfriend jealous is one of those ways and you can achieve that reaction through texts.

We are not saying that you send in messages saying you are out with someone else or that you are falling for a new guy. Although that is a sure way of making your ex-boyfriend jealous, it may also be a sure way of pushing him away. You would not want that. Instead, you may want to send in a text with a subtle message such as this:

"I went out with a friend today at Todd's, your favorite. Hope you are having a good day, too."

This text message leaves so much for imagination and interpretation. First, it did not say who the friend that the girl was referring to. Second, it did not say anything if it was a date or just a friendly hangout. And lastly, "Hope you are having a good day,

TOO" implies that the sender was having a great time with that "friend."

By sending this kind of text message, your ex-boyfriend will wonder who you are out with and what exactly is his standing in your life. So many thoughts will enter his mind upon receiving that text message. He will get confused because after reaching out to him, there you are going out with another person. He will get jealous and soon enough, you will receive a text message from him. His text will either clarify if that is a date or he will try to ask you out. Either way, you know you won because you successfully grabbed his attention.

Bringing out that green eyed monster in him will help you know if you guys actually have a shot in getting back together. The truth is this: if your ex-lover does not get jealous, he does not care that much anymore so trying to win him back might not be a good idea. But if he does show even a small hint of jealousy (even a sad Emoji would do!) then you are assured that you still have his attention and his heart!

Step Five: Do Not Play the Blame Game

In the third step, you are advised to reminisce with your ex-lover. However, this step is not without any limitations. Although it is nice to be reminded of the past, there are some parts of it which is better left alone, such as the break up.

Talking to your ex again will surely bring back some emotions which you have tried so hard to suppress. While you will mostly feel happy that you are communicating again, there is a big chance that you may also be reminded of the past, the pain and the misery that you experienced before. You may even want to start a fight just so you can prove yourself right. As tempting as that is, do not do it. The goal is to get back together with your ex and not to feed your ego.

Even if your guy starts acting all vulnerable and comfortable around you, do not take advantage of this by berating him with all that he did wrong in the past. Do not start pointing fingers.

When texting with your guy, avoid statements such as "The last few weeks would have been happy if you didn't leave" or "I hope you have learned your lesson by now." At all costs, do not start with the blame game.

This is a new start for the both of you. Trying to relieve the ugly parts of your relationship will not do both of you any good. Focus on the good ones instead and take it from there.

Step Six: End with Sweet Surrender

You and your ex-boyfriend have been affectionate with each other before. You were very much comfortable doing anything with him and you never felt awkward about talking about the silliest to the most serious things. In this last step to winning his heart back, this is what exactly you should do.

When you are getting back together with an ex-boyfriend, it is normal to keep your heart guarded because you are afraid of being rejected. Because you just had your heart broken, this is a normal reaction and it is completely understandable. However, if you have religiously followed steps one to five of this eBook, there is no need to fear anymore.

In the first step, you have made yourself a better person by keeping away from your guy for 30-days. This period was enough time to make him wonder and at the same time, this period was a good way for you to make yourself better.

In the second step, you did your best to be casual and cool. You made it seem like texting him does not have the end-goal of getting back together with him. By doing this, you were able to prove that you were not desperate in winning him back.

In the third and fifth step, you tried to relieve the past and avoided putting the blame into him. You were mature enough to accept that you guys have gone through a horrible break but you are willing to look beyond it. This showed that you have grown and that you are a mature person now.

In the fourth step, you brought out the Green Eyed monster in him and you were able to determine where you stand in his life. He got jealous and therefore, he still cares.

In this last step, you can now be assured that the last five steps have made it possible for you to act normal around your guy again.

Now that you have texted your way into consistency and a sense of normalcy, you may want to start being sweet with him again. It is now the time to put your guards down and end your game with relationship politics. At this point, you are now safe to text him with "I miss you" messages or those "I am lucky to have you" texts. It is also acceptable if you would text him invites into dates or hangouts, if you wish to do so. You can be as sweet, thoughtful and caring as you want to be. In this last step, there are no restrictions and limitations.

Also, if your guy responds to your sweet messages in the same way, you may also want to consider initiating the getting back together phase. Although you have successfully texted your way into winning your guy back, we advise that you formally get back together with him personally. Meet up for coffee or drinks and have "the talk". After all, starting over with an actual kiss is so much better than sealing the deal with an Emoji!

Finally Get Your Ex Back

I hope I have been able to help set you on the right path to getting your ex back. It can be a tough journey but if you feel that things were meant to be then putting the above steps into action and following through I have faith you can mend things and even make them better than before.

Now it's time to put the steps to work...

1 - **Don't Text Right Away, wait 30 days!** (This is so important but don't worry if you've already made contact, just stop right now)

By making sure you don't text him you'll keep him wondering and give yourself some time to clear your head.

2 - **After the Delay, Play it Casual and Cool**

After you survive that 30-day period, it is now time to text your ex-boyfriend. Play it cool and use the "bumped into" or "I discovered," type texts.

3 - **Bring up the Great Memories**

Now that you've got his interest, slowly bring up some of those great memories of the time before.

4 - **Get him a Little Jealous - Not a lot**

Use a text like: "I went out with a friend today at Todd's, your favorite. Hope you are having a good day, too." Leave something to the imagination.

5 - **Do Not Fall Victim to the Blame Game - Steer Clear!**

Remember, you're trying to get him back, not pick a fight. Keep those emotions in check and work on building something new and amazing.

6 - Seal the Deal :-)

Now that you've texted him back into your life, take the next step and see him in person. Drinks or coffee are a great place to start.

This checklist is broken down into an easy-to-manage process (well, as easy as a breakup and makeup can be).

Take it one step at a time and it won't be long 'til you have your ex back. All you have to do is be patient and take action. Yes, you'll need to put the effort in. But this effort will be rewarded with getting the man of your dreams back in your life.

Playing the slow and steady game gives you the best chance of showing him that you're the one and make him want you back more than ever. If you take these steps in proper order and take your time to introduce yourself back into your boyfriend's life through texting, it's totally possible to get him back.

Next thing you know he'll be back in your life! Now you have the plan on your side.

I wish you all the best in your success and happiness!

-James

Thank You

Before you go, I'd like to say "thank you" for purchasing my book.

You could have picked from dozens of books on relationship advice, but you took a chance to check out this one.

So a big thanks for purchasing this book and reading all the way the way through.

Now I'd like ask for a *small* favor. Could you please take a minute or two and leave a review for this book on Amazon.com.

This feedback will help me continue to write the kind of Kindle books that help you get results. And if you loved it, then please let me know :-)

Printed in Great Britain
by Amazon

17285404R00020